ULTIMATE HORSE & PONY COLOURING BOOK
COLOUR & LEARN

FANTASTIC ILLUSTRATIONS + FASCINATING FACTS & DESCRIPTIONS

Fantastic Illustrations, Fascinating Facts & Details

A Special Relationship
Man & Horse

The special relationship between man & horse began around 4000-3500 BC, when early humans encountered the wild equine ancestors of the horse. Initially these creatures were sought after for their meat and hides, providing sustenance and resources for survival. Yet, as time passed, a deeper understanding of the horse's potential unfolded.

Horses, with their strong frames and powerful legs, were soon used as transportation and to work alongside humans in the fields. They became the backbone of agriculture, revolutionising the way crops were grown and transported. This partnership propelled civilisations forward, leading to bountiful harvests and the growth of communities.

But it wasn't just in the fields that humans valued the horse. Their swiftness and grace led to a revolutionary shift in the way wars were fought. The emergence of cavalry units changed the very fabric of battle. These mounted warriors, armed with spears and bows, became unstoppable forces on the battlefield, shaping the outcomes of conflicts and influencing the fate of nations.

As societies expanded, horses became the driving force behind exploration and colonisation. They carried intrepid adventurers across uncharted territories, enabling the establishment of new lands and trade routes. The rhythmic sound of hooves echoed through history as horses forged connections between distant cultures, fostering the exchange of goods, ideas, and knowledge.

Amid the bustling activities of society, horses found their way into the hearts or many a man, their gentle presence providing solace & friendship, support & companionship.

Whilst in many modernised countries the horse is a symbol of tradition & recreation, there are still many cultures that depend on the power & grace of the noble & gentle horse.

Andalusian
The Pure Spanish Horse or Pura Raza Española

With a rich heritage intertwined with Spanish culture, the Andalusian horse, is a timeless symbol of grace and versatility, that boasts a distinct array of characteristics that have solidified its revered status in the equestrian world. With a harmonious blend of strength and elegance, this breed encapsulates centuries of history, cultural significance, and practical utility.

Standing at a compact yet powerful 15 to 16.2 hands high, the Andalusian's well-proportioned physique commands attention. Its strong, muscular build, often hidden beneath a flowing and wavy mane, imparts a sense of presence and nobility. The arched neck, expressive eyes, and refined head profile create an iconic silhouette that has captured the imagination of artists and enthusiasts alike.

The Andalusian's coat, can have many colours, including grey, bay, black, and chestnut. The breed does have a propensity for grey coats, changing from dark to grey over time, offers a striking contrast that highlights its regal demeanour.

Possessing smooth, elevated gaits, the breed is particularly suited for the artistry of classical dressage. This proficiency in collected, extended, and intricate manoeuvres is a testament to its innate intelligence and adaptability.

Temperamentally, the Andalusian is a gentle and noble, forming deep bonds with its human companions. Its willingness to please and eagerness to respond make it a delightful partner in various equestrian pursuits.

The Andalusian is extremely versatile. From historical roles as war horses and workhorses to modern achievements in dressage and jumping

Appaloosa
Distinctive Coat Patterns From The American West

The Appaloosa horse, renowned for its distinctive coat patterns and versatility, possesses a captivating combination of features that have made it a beloved and recognisable breed by equestrians.

Standing at varying heights, typically between 14.2 to 16 hands high, the Appaloosa boasts a sturdy and well-built frame that hints at its roots in the American West. Its muscular physique, often cloaked in a captivating spotted or mottled coat, lends an air of rugged elegance to the breed.

The most striking hallmark of the Appaloosa is its coat patterns. These patterns, which can range from leopard spots to roaning, express themselves in a remarkable array of colours and configurations. These distinct coat patterns, reminiscent of artwork, captivate the eye and contribute to the breed's allure.

Beneath its uniquely adorned exterior lies a horse with impressive movement. The Appaloosa's gaits are characterised by fluidity and agility, making it adept at various disciplines. Its adaptability shines in both Western and English riding, as well as in activities such as cutting, reining, and even endurance riding.

Temperamentally, the Appaloosa is known for its intelligence, gentle disposition, and strong work ethic. This breed often forms close bonds with its riders, displaying an eagerness to learn and a willingness to engage in various activities.

From its origins as a trusted companion of Native American tribes to its role in cattle work and ranching, the breed has excelled in numerous tasks.

The Appaloosa horse carries a historical and cultural significance. This breed, intertwined with Native American heritage and exploration of the American frontier, stands as a testament to the resilience and adaptability of the relationship between both horse and human.

Criollo
South American Survival & Exploration

The Criollo horse, a symbol of resilience and adaptability, possesses a remarkable array of characteristics that make it an integral part of South American culture and history. With its enduring spirit and versatility, the Criollo horse stands as a testament to the harmony between humans and their environment.

Standing at an average height of 13.2 to 14.2 hands high, the Criollo horse embodies a harmonious blend of strength and compactness. Its robust frame, shaped by generations of natural selection, reflects its ability to thrive in diverse and challenging landscapes.

One of the most distinctive features of the Criollo is its hardiness. Adapted to the rugged terrains and variable climates of South America, the Criollo horse possesses an innate ability to endure harsh conditions, making it a reliable partner for various activities.

The Criollo's coat comes in a range of natural colours, from bay and black to chestnut and grey.

The Criollo horse boasts impressive agility and stamina. Its gaits are smooth and balanced, allowing it to navigate uneven terrains and traverse long distances with ease. This endurance, coupled with its surefootedness, makes the Criollo an ideal choice for ranch work, herding, and trail riding.

Temperamentally, the Criollo horse has a calm and cooperative nature. Its strong bond with humans is rooted in its history as a working partner, showcasing an innate intelligence and a willingness to collaborate.

Culturally, the Criollo horse is deeply interwoven with the heritage of South American countries. It embodies the spirit of exploration & survival. The Criollo's legacy is a tribute to the resilience of indigenous peoples and their ability to thrive in challenging landscapes. Whether traversing mountains, guiding cattle, or competing in endurance races, the Criollo horse continues to capture the imagination and hearts of those who appreciate its timeless partnership and unwavering loyalty.

Dutch Warmblood
Athletic & Elegant

The Dutch Warmblood horse, a harmonious blend of elegance and athleticism, possesses a captivating combination of traits that have earned it a prominent place in the world of equestrian sports.

Standing at an average height of 15.2 to 17 hands high, the Dutch Warmblood has a real sense of presence and stature. Its well-proportioned build reflects a balance between strength and grace, making it a striking figure both in the show ring and in various equestrian disciplines.

The Dutch Warmblood's head, often adorned with a dished profile, adds to its refined appearance. Expressive eyes and well-shaped ears contribute to its noble countenance, reflecting a combination of intelligence and sensitivity.

The coat of the Dutch Warmblood comes in various colours, from solid to pinto patterns, highlighting its diversity and individuality. The breed's diverse coloration is often a reflection of its versatile pedigree, which draws from a range of European warmblood bloodlines.

Dutch Warmbloods are renowned for exceptional movement. Its gaits are characterised by fluidity, impulsion, and extension, qualities that make it a favoured choice for dressage and other high-level performance disciplines.

The breed has had significant achievements in the realm of dressage and show jumping, and has produced numerous champions and medallists at international competitions. Such as "Moorlands Totilas" who set records in dressage with rider Edward Gal, achieving three gold medals at the 2010 World Equestrian Games.

Dutch Warmbloods continues to capture the admiration and respect of riders, trainers, and enthusiasts worldwide.

Hanoverian
Epitome of elegance and athleticism

The Hanoverian horse, an epitome of elegance and athleticism, possesses a remarkable blend of traits that have established it as a premier sport horse breed.

Standing at an average height of 15.3 to 17.2 hands high, the Hanoverian horse commands attention with its impressive stature and well-proportioned frame.

The Hanoverian's head is often characterised by expressive eyes, a straight profile, and well-shaped ears. This contributes to its overall balanced and harmonious appearance.

The breed's movement is a sight to behold. The Hanoverian's gaits are characterised by elegance, fluidity, and impulsion. With a strong emphasis on dressage, the breed excels in performing collected and extended movements, showcasing its natural athleticism and responsiveness.

The Hanoverian horse is known for its trainable and willing nature. Its intelligence and cooperative spirit make it an ideal partner for riders across various levels of experience.

One of the most notable achievements of the Hanoverian breed lies in its impressive record of success in the world of equestrian sports. Hanoverians have garnered numerous medals and accolades in disciplines such as dressage, show jumping, and eventing.

Icelandic
Tölt & Flying Pace

The Icelandic horse, a living symbol of Iceland's history and culture, possesses a captivating blend of traits that make it a unique and cherished breed.

With an average height of 13 to 14 hands high, the Icelandic horse is compact yet sturdy, reflecting its ability to navigate the challenging landscapes of Iceland. Its thick coat and bushy mane and tail offer protection against the harsh weather conditions that characterise its native land.

One of the most remarkable features of the Icelandic horse is its unique gaits. In addition to the walk, trot, and canter, the breed possesses two additional gaits: the tölt and the flying pace. The tölt is a smooth, four-beat gait that provides a comfortable and swift ride, while the flying pace is a rapid, two-beat gait used for racing.

The Icelandic horse is known for its friendly and sociable nature. Its strong bond with humans is nurtured by the breed's close interactions with people, as Icelandic horses are often treated as family members rather than mere animals.

The Icelandic horse is deeply rooted in the history and traditions of Iceland. It played a crucial role in the settlement of the island and has been a faithful companion to generations of Icelanders. Today, the breed remains an integral part of Icelandic culture, celebrated in festivals, competitions, and daily life.

In terms of achievements, the Icelandic horse has made its mark on the international stage as well. It has earned recognition for its performance in various equestrian events, particularly in gaited disciplines. While specific medals and achievements may vary, the breed's unique abilities have garnered respect and admiration in competitions around the world.

New Zealand Clydesdale
Majestic & Powerful

The New Zealand Clydesdale horse, a majestic and powerful breed that embodies a blend of strength and grace.

Standing at an impressive height of 16 to 18 hands high, the New Zealand Clydesdale is a true equine giant that commands attention. Its robust and muscular build is a testament to its heritage as a workhorse, capable of tackling demanding tasks on the farm and in other practical settings.

One of the defining features of the New Zealand Clydesdale is its majestic appearance. With its feathered legs, flowing mane, and expressive eyes, the breed exudes an air of regal elegance that harks back to its European ancestry.

The New Zealand Clydesdale's coat comes in various solid colours, often showcasing rich and earthy tones that complement its sturdy physique. This coat, along with its striking white facial blaze, creates a distinctive and recognisable appearance.

The New Zealand Clydesdale horse possesses remarkable strength and a gentle disposition. Its patient and cooperative nature makes it well-suited for farm work, logging, and other labour-intensive tasks.

The breed's versatility is evident in its ability to excel in a range of activities. From pulling heavy loads to participating in parades and shows, the New Zealand Clydesdale's adaptability is a testament to its enduring spirit and willingness to engage in various roles.

Palomino American Quarter Horse
Skillful In The Rodeo Arena

The Palomino American Quarter Horse, a radiant blend of beauty and athleticism, boasts a striking combination of features that have earned it a place of distinction in the equestrian world.

Standing at an average height of 14 to 16 hands high, the Palomino Quarter Horse possesses a compact yet powerfully built frame that hints at its Quarter Horse lineage. Its muscular physique is adorned by a lustrous and golden palomino coat. Its radiant gold hue, ranging from pale champagne to deep amber, creates a dazzling display that is further accentuated by an often white flowing mane and tail.

Beyond its striking appearance, the Palomino Quarter Horse is a wonderful example of athleticism. With a natural aptitude for speed and agility, it excels in a variety of disciplines, including barrel racing, reining, cutting, and pleasure riding. Its versatility and performance capabilities have made it a popular choice among riders seeking both style and substance.

Temperamentally, the Palomino Quarter Horse embodies the quintessential traits of the American Quarter Horse breed—intelligence, willingness, and a strong work ethic. Its cooperative nature and quick learning ability make it a sought-after partner in both competitive arenas and leisurely rides.

Palomino Quarter Horses have achieved acclaim in disciplines like reining, where their skill has dazzled audiences and judges alike. Their performance in rodeo events, such as barrel racing and roping, highlights their adaptability and competitive spirit.

Mustang
A Symbol Of The American Frontier

The Mustang, is considered a symbol of freedom and untamed spirit, possesses a captivating array of characteristics that reflect its wild origins and indomitable nature. With its historical significance, resilience, and contemporary achievements, the Mustang stands as a symbol of the American frontier.

Standing at various heights due to its diverse ancestry, the Mustang is characterised by a sturdy and compact frame that shouts of its ability to thrive in the rugged landscapes of North America. Its well-adapted physique reflects generations of survival in challenging environments.

The most iconic feature of the Mustang is its unbridled and natural beauty. Displaying an array of coat colours and patterns, from solid to spotted and everything in between, the Mustang's coat is a living canvas that tells the story of its ancestry and free-roaming existence.

The Mustang's has a swift, agile gait and a powerful stride, it navigates varied terrains with grace and ease. This natural athleticism and surefootedness are a direct reflection of the challenges its ancestors overcame in the untamed wilderness.

Mustangs have independent and curious spirits. Its inherent wariness, forged through generations of survival instincts, speaks to its keen awareness of its surroundings and its ability to adapt to changing circumstances.

One of the most poignant aspects of the Mustang's legacy is its historical connection to the American frontier. Descended from horses brought by Spanish explorers and settlers, the Mustang became a symbol of the untamed West, capturing the imagination of pioneers, cowboys, and adventurers.

Many famous tales and stories have been told about the mustang and its intrepid character.

Palomino
Golden Elegance

The Palomino, is a living embodiment of golden elegance, possesses a set of captivating traits that have made it a beloved and iconic breed. With its distinctive coat colour and versatile nature, its easily recognisable.

Standing at various heights, typically between 14 to 17 hands high, the Palomino's stature is well-proportioned on its frame.

The hallmark of the Palomino horse is its stunning coat colour. Ranging from a pale, creamy hue to a rich, deep gold, the Palomino's coat shimmers like sunlight on a field of wheat. Its lustrous mane and tail, often flowing and wavy.

The Palomino's movements are characterised by fluidity and agility, making it a versatile and sought-after breed in a variety of disciplines. Its versatility extends to Western riding, dressage, trail riding, and even show jumping.

The Palomino's temperament is equally charming, known for its gentle disposition and strong bond with humans. This breed often forms close connections with its riders, making it an excellent partner in various equestrian pursuits.

One of the most famous stories within the Palomino breed revolves around Roy Rogers' horse, Trigger. Trigger, a golden Palomino with a distinct white blaze on his forehead, became a symbol of Western film and television. The legendary horse starred alongside Roy Rogers in countless movies and TV shows, captivating audiences with his stunning appearance and intelligence.

Swedish WarmBlood
Elegant & Athletic

The Swedish Warmblood, is adescribed as a harmonious blend of elegance and athleticism, that possesses a captivating combination of traits that have established it as a prized and versatile breed.

Standing at an average height of 16 to 17 hands high, the Swedish Warmblood horse presents a well-proportioned and powerful physique. Its conformation reflects meticulous breeding efforts aimed at producing a horse suitable for various disciplines and equestrian pursuits.

Characterised by its refined head, expressive eyes, and intelligent demeanour, the Swedish Warmblood embodies the essence of equine grace. Its athletic build, with a strong back and hindquarters, conveys both strength and agility—an ideal combination for a wide range of equestrian endeavours.

The Swedish Warmblood's coat can vary in color, often including bay, chestnut, black, and grey. This diversity is a reflection of the breed's diverse genetic pool, contributing to its aesthetic appeal and adaptability.

The Swedish Warmblood is celebrated for its exceptional movement. Its gaits are marked by fluidity, extension, and engagement, making it a favored choice in dressage, show jumping, eventing, and other competitive disciplines. It has many successes on the global equestrian stage. Swedish Warmblood horses have secured numerous medals in international competitions.

American Paint Horse
Colourful & Versatile

The American Paint Horse, are a canvas of colour and versatility, . With its distinctive coat patterns, rich history, and remarkable achievements, the American Paint Horse embodies the spirit of diversity and partnership.

Standing at varying heights, typically ranging from 14 to 16 hands high, the American Paint Horse presents a striking and eye-catching presence. Its well-proportioned build, defined by strength and agility, is accentuated by its uniquely patterned coat, making it a breed that stands out in any setting.

Usual coat patterns include overo and tobiano variations, which create a breathtaking tapestry of colors and shapes. From striking contrast to elegantly blended hues, the coat patterns of the American Paint Horse make each horse very individual..

Their history is rooted in a fusion of Spanish horse breeding and Native American horsemanship. With ancestry tracing back to the horses brought to the Americas by Spanish explorers, the breed's distinctive markings emerged through generations of careful selection and natural variation.

The American Paint Horse's achievements extend to the competitive arena. With a legacy of medals and titles, these horses have made their mark in rodeos, reining competitions, and a wide range of events.

Trakehner
Prize Winning Intelligence

Trakehner horse, a breed renowned for its elegance, athleticism, and rich history, it has a status as a prized and versatile equine partner. With a legacy deeply rooted in purposeful breeding and a notable presence in the world of equestrian sports.

Standing at a height of 15.2 to 17 hands high, the Trakehner is a true example of refined and well-proportioned physique. Its lean and athletic build, characterised by a graceful neck, strong back, and expressive eyes, reflects the meticulous breeding practices that have shaped the breed over centuries.

The origins of the Trakehner trace back to the East Prussian region, where local horsemen sought to create a versatile and enduring horse. Through careful selection and crossing of various breeds, including Arabians, Thoroughbreds, and native stock, the Trakehner emerged as a distinct and prized breed. The breed's founders envisioned a horse that would excel in various disciplines, from carriage driving and dressage to hunting and general riding.

One of the hallmarks of the Trakehner is its elegant movement. With flowing gaits characterised by suspension and impulsion, the Trakehner's athleticism and ability to collect make it a sought-after choice for dressage. Its versatile nature extends to other equestrian disciplines as well, including show jumping and eventing.

There are many famous examples of the Trakehner breed. Including "Abdullah," a Trakehner-Thoroughbred cross. "Gribaldi," a Trakehner stallion, who excelled in dressage. But later gained prominence through his offspring, which included the legendary dressage stallion "Totilas," who achieved unprecedented success under the rider Edward Gal, capturing multiple world records and championship titles.

Clydesdale
Majestic, Powerful & Iconic

The Clydesdale horse, is a majestic and iconic breed, possesses distinct characteristics and a rich history that have solidified its place as a symbol of strength and elegance.

Clydesdales are tall, at an average height of 16 to 18 hands high, the Clydesdale commands attention with its imposing stature and sturdy build. Its muscular frame, with broad shoulders, a deep chest, and powerful hindquarters, portrays a sense of raw strength and capability.

The Clydesdale's most recognisable feature aside from its size, is its feathered legs, where long hair covers the lower legs and creates a distinct appearance.

Originating from the banks of the River Clyde in Scotland, the Clydesdale horse has a rich heritage deeply intertwined with agricultural pursuits. Bred for heavy farm work, it played a crucial role in plowing fields, hauling timber, and transporting goods, contributing to the economic and agricultural development of its region.

One of the most famous examples of Clydesdale horses is the Budweiser Clydesdales, a team of horses that has become an enduring symbol of the Budweiser beer brand. These horses, meticulously bred and trained, showcase the breed's strength and elegance as they pull elaborately decorated wagons in parades and events around the world.

Beyond their role in advertising, Clydesdales have achieved recognition in various competitive and ceremonial contexts. They have participated in prestigious horse shows and competitions, showcasing their abilities in driving, heavy pulling, and draft classes. Their impressive size and grace make them a popular choice for carriage rides and ceremonial events.

Welsh Pony
Gentle Disposition & Manageable Size

The Welsh Pony and Cob is a group of four closely-related horse breeds including both pony and cob types, which originated in Wales in the United Kingdom.

With a height of 11 to 13.2 hands high, the Welsh Pony boasts a compact yet sturdy frame that belies its remarkable capabilities. It has a well-proportioned albeit smaller build.

The Welsh Pony is the result of careful breeding, with a lineage that can be traced back to ancient times. This breed developed in the Welsh hills and valleys, where its hardy nature was honed by centuries of living in challenging environments. The selective breeding practices aimed at enhancing specific traits led to the creation of four distinct sections: Section A, B, C, and D, each with unique characteristics and uses.

In the realm of equestrian achievements, the Welsh Pony has left an indelible mark. Its agility and versatility have made it a popular choice for various disciplines, from riding and driving to jumping and eventing. The breed's innate intelligence and willingness to learn have paved the way for numerous success stories in competitive arenas.

Famous examples of Welsh Ponies have made their mark on the international stage. One such example is Nerwyn Llwynog, a Welsh Pony stallion that captured hearts with his exceptional jumping prowess and striking presence. Another notable figure is Cusop Jovial, whose remarkable dressage skills and harmonious partnership with his rider garnered widespread admiration.

In addition to these achievements, the Welsh Pony's versatility extends to its role as an ideal mount for young riders. Its gentle disposition and manageable size make it an excellent choice for introducing children to the joys of riding, fostering a lifelong love for horses.

Carriage-Type Oldenburg
Bred For Carriage Driving

The Oldenburg or Oldenburger is a warmblood horse from the northwestern corner of Lower Saxony, what was formerly the Grand Duchy of Oldenburg. The breed was built on a mare base of all-purpose farm and carriage horses, today called the Alt-Oldenburger.

Standing at an imposing height, typically between 16 to 17 hands high, the Oldenburg carriage horse commands attention with its majestic presence. Its stature, coupled with a strong and muscular build, reflects its historical role as a symbol of aristocracy and grandeur.

The Oldenburg carriage horse's origins trace back to the Oldenburg region of Germany, where it was selectively bred to excel in carriage driving. Its rich heritage is a product of meticulous breeding, combining the strength and power of draft horses with the elegance and refinement of lighter breeds.

One of the hallmark features of the Oldenburg is its exceptional movement. Characterized by fluid, ground-covering gaits, the breed's ability to exhibit extended trot and graceful action makes it ideally suited for the art of carriage driving. This harmonious combination of athleticism and grace defines the Oldenburg's allure.

Beyond its physical attributes, the Oldenburg carriage horse exudes a calm and cooperative temperament. Its willingness to perform intricate maneuvers and its responsiveness to subtle cues reflect the deep bond between horse and driver, essential for successful carriage competitions.

The Oldenburg carriage horse has achieved acclaim on the international stage, earning medals and accolades in prestigious driving events. It has garnered attention for its impressive turnout and impeccable performance, showcasing the harmonious partnership between horse, driver, and carriage.

One notable example is the renowned Oldenburg stallion "Limelight," who achieved international success in combined driving events. Limelight's exceptional performance and ability to navigate challenging obstacles underscore the breed's aptitude for carriage driving.

Latvian Horse
Adaptable Baltic Work-Horse

The Latvian Horse, a testament to Latvia's equestrian heritage and rural traditions, showcases a unique blend of characteristics that reflect its origins and role within the Baltic country. With its hardy constitution and historical significance, the Latvian Horse stands as a living tribute to the nation's enduring bond with these majestic creatures.

Standing at an average height of 14 to 15 hands high, the Latvian Horse possesses a sturdy and well-proportioned frame that embodies its adaptability to the region's varying landscapes. Its robust build, defined by generations of selective breeding.

At the heart of the Latvian Horse's appeal lies its exceptional adaptability. Bred to withstand the demands of both agricultural labour and recreational riding, this breed has proven its versatility time and again. Its strength, combined with a calm and cooperative temperament, has made it an ideal choice for a variety of equestrian pursuits.

One of the hallmarks of the Latvian Horse is its unique coat colour, often seen in shades of dun or grey. This coloration not only reflects the breed's historical ties to the Latvian landscape but also contributes to its distinctive appearance.

The breeding of the Latvian Horse is a reflection of Latvia's agrarian past. Developed through a combination of local horse breeds and influences from neighbouring countries, the Latvian Horse showcases a careful blend of traits that suit its role as a versatile work and riding companion.

The breed's achievements are a testament to its capabilities. In Latvia's rural communities, the Latvian Horse has long been a reliable partner in agricultural activities, ranging from plowing fields to hauling timber. Moreover, the breed has made its mark in equestrian sports, with Latvian Horses excelling in disciplines such as dressage, show jumping, and eventing.

American Saddlebred
The First American Breed

The American Saddlebred, is the embodiment of elegance and versatility, it possesses a unique array of traits that have solidified its esteemed position.

Standing at a height ranging from 15 to 17 hands, the American Saddlebred showcases a well-proportioned and balanced build. Its sleek and arched neck, accentuated by a graceful carriage, contributes to an aura of regal presence. This breed's innate elegance is further enhanced by its luxuriant, flowing mane and tail, adding to its visual allure.

Bred with a focus on versatility and performance, the American Saddlebred is renowned for its three distinct gaits: the slow gait, the rack, and the animated trot. These natural gaits, finely honed through generations of selective breeding, are a testament to the breed's adaptability and artful development.

In the realm of achievements, the American Saddlebred has captured hearts and accolades alike. Its exceptional talent and graceful movements have made it a fixture in various equestrian disciplines, including saddle seat, driving, and even dressage. The breed's innate ability to captivate audiences is often showcased in the show ring, where it exudes an aura of sophistication and poise.

Notable achievements in the American Saddlebred's history include its recognition as the first American breed, as well as its contributions to the development of the Tennessee Walking Horse and the Missouri Fox Trotter. The American Saddlebred's legacy is also intertwined with the growth of American horsemanship, marking its significance in the nation's equestrian heritage.

Famous examples within the breed have left an indelible mark on the equestrian world. "Sultan's Great Day" stands as a revered example, earning the Triple Crown of the American Saddlebred industry. The stallion "CH Wing Commander" left an enduring legacy with his numerous championships, displaying the breed's prowess in the show ring.

Holsteiner
The Oldest Of Warmblood Breeds

The Holsteiner is a breed of horse originating in the Schleswig-Holstein region of northern Germany. It is thought to be the oldest of warmblood breeds, tracing back to the 13th century. Though the population is not large, Holsteiners are a dominant force of international show jumping, and are found at the top levels of dressage, combined driving, show hunters, and eventing.

With a height ranging from 16 to 17 hands high, the Holsteiners selective breeding for both strength and grace is evident. Its robust and muscular frame, often complemented by shades of bay, chestnut, black, or grey coats, exemplifies its harmonious combination of form and function.

At the heart of the Holsteiner's excellence lies its breeding. The breed's history is rooted in the breeding of war horses and carriage horses, a lineage that demanded both power and elegance. Over time, the Holsteiner has evolved into an esteemed sport horse, particularly excelling in show jumping and dressage disciplines.

The Holsteiner's remarkable aptitude for jumping has earned it a reputation as one of the world's premier jumping breeds. It has consistently proven its mettle on the international stage, capturing the hearts of equestrian enthusiasts and garnering admiration for its incredible jumping prowess.

Among the ranks of Holsteiner excellence, certain individuals have etched their names into the record books. Take, for instance, Lettie Teague, a Holsteiner mare who clinched a gold medal at the 1968 Mexico City Olympics under the skilled guidance of rider William Steinkraus. This achievement marked a defining moment for the breed's prowess in international competition.

In more recent times, the Holsteiner stallion Hickstead, affectionately known as "The Stallion of the Century," has left an indelible mark on the sport of show jumping. Under the masterful riding of Eric Lamaze, Hickstead secured numerous victories, including a gold medal at the 2008 Beijing Olympics and multiple wins in prestigious Grand Prix events.

Mecklenburger
Calm & Willing Learner

The Mecklenburger is a warmblood horse bred in the Mecklenburg-Vorpommern region of north-eastern Germany.

With an average height of 15.2 to 16.2 hands high, the Mecklenburger horse is a harmonious blend of refinement and strength, making it a captivating presence in various equestrian disciplines.

The origins of the Mecklenburger breed can be traced back to the Mecklenburg-Vorpommern region of Germany. The breed's development was guided by a meticulous breeding program that aimed to combine the qualities of the Holsteiner, Hanoverian, and Thoroughbred breeds. This deliberate blending has resulted in a horse that excels in both performance and temperament.

One of the hallmark features of the Mecklenburger is its versatile abilities. With its strong conformation and athletic build, the breed is well-suited for a wide range of disciplines, including dressage, show jumping, eventing, and even driving. This adaptability has earned the Mecklenburger a reputation as a reliable and competent partner in various equestrian endeavours.

Temperamentally, the Mecklenburger horse exudes a calm and willing nature. Its intelligent and trainable disposition makes it a favourite among riders and trainers alike, as it readily absorbs new skills and eagerly participates in training.

The Mecklenburger breed's achievements have garnered attention on both national and international stages. These horses have earned medals and accolades in various equestrian competitions, showcasing their prowess in the arena. Their success is a testament to the breed's combination of athleticism, elegance, and train-ability.

Zangersheide
Bred For Capability Instead Of Bloodline

The Zangersheide is a Belgian breed or stud-book of warmblood sport horses. It is one of three Belgian warmblood breeds or stud-books, the others being the Belgian Sport Horse and the Belgian Warmblood.

Standing at an average height of 16 to 17 hands high, its balanced physique reflects careful breeding. The breed's strong bone structure and refined features create a harmonious and eye-catching appearance.

Central to the Zangersheide's allure is its remarkable breeding philosophy. Established as a studbook in the mid-20th century, Zangersheide focused on selecting horses based on their performance capabilities rather than strict adherence to traditional bloodlines. This approach, centred around performance rather than pedigree, has led to the creation of a breed known for its versatility, agility, and competitive spirit.

The Zangersheide horse's coat colour is often diverse, with bay, chestnut, grey, and black being common variations. This wide range of colours is down to the breed's diverse genetic pool and its emphasis on performance over aesthetics.

The Zangersheide's athleticism shines through in its movement. With powerful and fluid gaits, the breed excels in a variety of disciplines, including show jumping, dressage, eventing, and more.

Notable examples of Zangersheide horses have achieved remarkable success on the international stage. Their accomplishments include:

Ratina Z: A legendary show jumper, Ratina Z won numerous Grand Prix titles and claimed back-to-back Olympic silver medals in 1992 and 1996.

&

Sapphire: This exceptional mare, ridden by McLain Ward, earned an Olympic gold medal in 2004 and was a dominant force in the show jumping world.

Westphalian
Exceptional Jumping & Dressage Abilities

The Westphalian or Westfalen is a warmblood horse bred in the Westphalia region of western Germany. The Westphalian is closely affiliated with the state-owned stud farm of Warendorf, which it shares with the Rhinelander. Since World War II, the Westphalian horse has been bred to the same standard as the other German warmbloods, and they are particularly famous as Olympic-level show jumpers and dressage horses.

Standing between 16 to 17 hands high, the Westphalian is the result of meticulous efforts of breeders to craft a horse that excels in both form and function.

At the heart of the Westphalian's excellence lies its carefully managed breeding program. Rooted in the Westphalia region of Germany, breeders have meticulously selected bloodlines to create a horse with exceptional jumping and dressage abilities. This deliberate approach has given rise to a breed known for its athleticism, trainability, and competitive edge.

The Westphalian's coat, ranges from solid colours like bay, brown, and chestnut to occasional grey, showcases the breed's classic and versatile appearance. This colour palette highlights the breed's adaptability and suitability for various disciplines.

Beyond its physical attributes, the Westphalian horse shines in the arena. Its gaits are characterised by suppleness, impulsion, and rhythm, making it an ideal contender in both dressage and show jumping. The breed's natural talent for these disciplines has led to a string of achievements and medals on national and international stages.

One of the most famous examples of the Westphalian breed is "Ratina Z," a mare that achieved remarkable success in show jumping. Under the guidance of rider Ludger Beerbaum, Ratina Z secured multiple Olympic and World Championship medals, etching her name into the annals of equestrian history.

Brabant - Belgian Draught
The Strongest Horse In The World

The Belgian Draught, Dutch: Belgisch Trekpaard, French: Trait belge, is a Belgian breed of draught horse. It originates in the region of the Low Countries that is now central Belgium, and may also be called the Brabant after the former Province of Brabant in that area. The massive and muscular Belgian Draught is the strongest horse breed in the world.

Standing tall with a robust and muscular frame, the Brabant horse commands attention with its impressive stature. A product of careful breeding, it typically stands between 16 to 17 hands high, showcasing a harmonious balance between strength and elegance.

Originating in the Brabant region of Belgium, this breed's lineage is rooted in a meticulous selection process. The Brabant horse's breeding has focused on enhancing its capabilities as a draft horse, resulting in a powerful and dependable partner for heavy labour and agricultural tasks.

Distinctive in appearance, the Brabant horse boasts a thickset neck, a broad chest, and powerful hindquarters. These features, meticulously honed through generations of breeding, underscore the breed's proficiency in pulling heavy loads and performing arduous farm work.

The Brabant horse's contributions extend beyond the fields, as it has excelled in various competitions and events. Renowned for its pulling prowess, the Brabant has excelled in draft horse competitions, showcasing its strength and teamwork in events such as pulling contests and plowing matches.

Famous examples of the Brabant breed include notable achievements in both competitions and historical contexts. In the early 20th century, a Brabant stallion named "Prince Pat" earned acclaim for his exceptional pulling abilities, garnering multiple awards and medals for his remarkable feats of strength.

Morgan
From the stallion "Figure"

The Morgan is one of the earliest horse breeds developed in the United States

Standing at an average height of 14.1 to 15.2 hands high, the Morgan horse is well-proportioned with a muscular frame, enhanced by a gracefully arched neck.

The lineage of the Morgan horse traces back to a single foundation sire, a stallion named Figure, whose legacy laid the groundwork for the breed's distinctive attributes. Characterised by a compact yet powerful physique, the Morgan's conformation reflects its heritage of versatility and work ethic.

Morgan horses are renowned for their exceptional movement. They possess fluid and balanced gaits that make them adept performers in various disciplines. Their versatility shines in everything from driving and dressage to jumping and trail riding, showcasing their adaptability and willingness to excel.

The Morgan horse is known for its intelligence, gentle disposition, and strong bond with humans. This affinity for forming deep connections fosters a sense of partnership that is essential for success in any equestrian pursuit.

The breed's history is studded with tales of achievement and accomplishment. One notable figure is Justin Morgan, a schoolteacher and composer for whom the breed's foundation sire is named. The legendary endurance, strength, and character of Justin Morgan's horse, Figure, became the prototype for the breed's exceptional qualities.

Stories of the Morgan horse's feats and achievements are woven into the fabric of American equestrian history. From serving as cavalry mounts in the Civil War to excelling in modern-day dressage and driving competitions.

Marwari
Indian Elegance

The Marwari horse, a captivating symbol of Indian heritage and elegance, possesses a unique array of characteristics that set it apart as a distinctive and cherished breed. The breed has distinctive appearance, historical significance, and notable achievements.

Standing at an average height of 14 to 15 hands, the Marwari horse showcases an air of refinement and regality. Its well-proportioned physique, defined by a slightly arched neck and finely chiselled head, captures the essence of grace and beauty.

One of the most striking and recognisable features of the Marwari is its distinctively curved ears, which can rotate 180 degrees. These elegant ears add to the breed's allure and lend it an air of enigmatic charm.

The Marwari's coat, often found in shades of bay, grey, chestnut, and palomino, further contributes to its captivating presence. This range of colors showcases the breed's adaptability to the diverse landscapes of its native India.

Bred in the arid and challenging regions of Rajasthan, India, the Marwari horse has developed exceptional hardiness and endurance. Its ability to navigate rugged terrains and endure extreme weather conditions reflects its ancestral connection with the desert landscape.

The Marwari's movement is elegant and fluid. Its ability to perform intricate maneuvers, such as the passage and piaffe, makes it a sought-after breed for traditional Indian equestrian arts and modern disciplines alike.

Historically, the Marwari horse has been closely intertwined with Rajput culture and royalty. It was favored by Maharajas and warriors for its bravery, speed, and versatility in battle.

In recent times, the Marwari horse has gained recognition beyond India's borders. It has participated in various equestrian competitions and events, showcasing its talent and potential on an international stage.

Lipizzaner
Spanish Dancer

The Lipizzaner breed is steeped in history, elegance, and exceptional achievements. With a focus on its breeding, notable individuals, and remarkable accomplishments.. This breed, known for its stunning presence and remarkable abilities, traces its origins back to the royal court of the Habsburg Monarchy.

Lipizzaners stand at an average height of 14.2 to 15.2 hands high, the Lipizzaner's compact and elegant physique is regal & refined. Its noble head, framed by a well-arched neck, showcases an expressive face.

The signature coat colour of the Lipizzaner is a luminous shade of white, accentuating its captivating presence. However, these horses are born dark and gradually develop their characteristic white coats over time. This colour transformation adds to their mystique and allure.

The Lipizzaner's breeding is a labor of love, a testament to the meticulous efforts of generations of breeders. The breed's roots can be traced back to the 16th century Lipica Stud Farm in modern-day Slovenia, where the Spanish Andalusian, Arabian, and Berber bloodlines were meticulously blended to create this exquisite equine.

One of the most renowned achievements associated with the Lipizzaner horse is its affiliation with the Spanish Riding School in Vienna, Austria. The school, established in the 18th century, is famed for its classical dressage training and performances that highlight the breed's natural aptitude for haute école movements.

Perhaps the most iconic event in the Lipizzaner's legacy is the "Airs Above the Ground," a series of breathtaking leaps and manoeuvres that include the capriole, courbette, and levade. These awe-inspiring movements demonstrate the horse's exceptional strength, agility, and willingness to perform, captivating audiences worldwide.

Australian Stock
From Down Under

The Australian Stock Horse, a quintessential icon of Australian rural heritage, possesses a distinct set of qualities that highlight its vital role in the country's agricultural history.

Standing at an average height of 14.2 to 16 hands high, the Australian Stock Horse is a blend of strength and agility. Its well-defined muscles and sturdy build reflect its origins as a working horse, adapted to handle the challenges of the Australian outback.

The Australian Stock Horse owes its lineage to a diverse mix of breeds, including Thoroughbreds, Arabians, and British pony breeds. This careful blending was aimed at creating a horse that could excel in cattle work and perform under the demanding conditions of rural Australia.

One of the most remarkable attributes of the Australian Stock Horse is its legendary endurance. This breed's ability to work tirelessly for hours on end, herding cattle and traversing vast distances, speaks volumes about its strength and stamina.

The coat of the Australian Stock Horse varies, showcasing an array of colours including bay, chestnut, black, and grey. This practical and hardy coloration reflects its role as a utilitarian horse, ready to tackle any task thrown its way.

Beyond its physical characteristics, the Australian Stock Horse is celebrated for its intelligence and cooperative nature. Its close partnership with stock-men and farmers in the demanding world of livestock management has forged a deep understanding between horse and rider.

The Australian Stock Horse's versatility is legendary. From mustering cattle on expansive stations to competing in rodeos and camp drafting events, this breed is the embodiment of adaptability and skill.

One of the most famous Australian Stock Horses is "Rivoli Ray," an exceptional stallion that achieved legendary status in camp drafting competitions.

Missouri Fox Trotter
Smooth Rider

The Missouri Fox Trotter is celebrated for its unique gait and versatility, it is an exceptional American breed.

Standing between 14 to 16 hands high, the Missouri Fox Trotter boasts an athletic build that seamlessly combines strength and elegance on its well-proportioned frame.

One of the Missouri Fox Trotter's most distinguishing features is its exceptional gait. The "fox trot", It is an ambling gait that has a four-beat broken diagonal step where the front foot of the diagonal pair lands before the hind, eliminating the moment of suspension and increasing smoothness. This unique gait offers a comfortable and efficient ride, making it a favoured choice for both leisurely trail rides and long journeys.

The breed's development can be traced back to the Ozark Mountains of Missouri. Through a careful blending of various breeds, including the Tennessee Walking Horse, Arabian, Morgan, and Standardbred, the Missouri Fox Trotter was crafted to possess its distinct gait while retaining its versatility and adaptability.

The Missouri Fox Trotter's coat comes in a variety of colours, from solid shades to striking patterns. This diverse palette adds to its allure and showcases the breed's visual appeal.

In addition to its exceptional gait, the Missouri Fox Trotter exhibits an amiable and willing temperament. Its intelligence and cooperative nature make it a trusted partner in various equestrian activities.

The breed's versatility extends to a wide range of disciplines. From trail riding and endurance races to ranch work and even show arenas, the Missouri Fox Trotter excels in diverse roles, reflecting its well-rounded abilities.

Percheron
Strong & Graceful

The Percheron horse, a majestic symbol of strength and elegance, possesses a captivating array of qualities that have made it a powerhouse within the equestrian world. With a heritage steeped in history and a legacy of remarkable achievements.

Percheron stand tall at an average height of 16 to 17.2 hands high, Its sturdy, muscular frame is a reflection of centuries of selective breeding, resulting in a breed renowned for its immense strength and versatility.

Originating in the Perche region of France, the Percheron's history dates back to medieval times. Bred primarily for heavy farm labour and draft work, these horses played an essential role in plowing fields, pulling carts, and transporting goods. This historical connection to agriculture has contributed to the breed's enduring work ethic and willingness to undertake challenging tasks.

The Percheron's coat can range from solid black and grey to bay and roan, adding to its allure. Its thick mane and tail, often contrasted against its sleek body, create a visual harmony that is both captivating and dignified.

In terms of movement, the Percheron showcases impressive grace and fluidity despite its size. Its gaits are surprisingly light and agile for a draft breed, which has led to its utilisation in various equestrian activities beyond traditional heavy work.

The Percheron's legacy is marked by a remarkable dedication to breeding for excellence. In the early 19th century, efforts were made to refine the breed, resulting in the "English type" Percheron, which displayed increased elegance and a more refined appearance. These selective breeding practices have led to the creation of a breed that excels not only in strength but also in beauty and adaptability.

Famous Percheron examples include "Billy," a Percheron who gained international acclaim by pulling a 45-ton, 40-foot-long road train in Australia. This remarkable feat earned him a place in the Guinness World Records.

Paso Fino
Unique Footfall Pattern

The Paso Fino is a naturally gaited light horse breed dating back to horses imported to the Caribbean from Spain. Pasos are prized for their smooth, natural, four-beat, lateral ambling gait and this sets it apart from other breeds.

Standing at an average height of 13.2 to 15.2 hands high, the Paso Fino horse possesses a balanced and well-proportioned frame. Its refined physique, often accentuated by a luxuriously flowing mane and tail, exudes an air of grace and poise.

The hallmark of the Paso Fino is its distinctive gait, known as the "Paso Fino". This four-beat lateral gait is incredibly smooth and rhythmic, offering riders an unparalleled level of comfort and control. The unique footfall pattern, characterised by each foot hitting the ground independently, creates an almost dance-like motion that sets the Paso Fino apart from other breeds.

The origins of the Paso Fino can be traced back to Spain, where the Andalusian, Barb, and Spanish Jennet breeds played pivotal roles in its development. Through generations of selective breeding, the Paso Fino's unique gait was refined and perfected, resulting in a horse that combines both elegance and functionality.

The Paso Fino's versatility extends beyond its gait. It is known for its gentle disposition, intelligence, and willingness to please. This combination of attributes makes it a popular choice not only for pleasure riding but also for various equestrian disciplines, including trail riding, endurance, and even dressage.

Shetland Pony
Greatness In A Small Package

The Shetland pony, a charming and hardy breed, with its diminutive size and remarkable strength, the Shetland pony is a unique but endearing breed.

Standing at the short height of 7 to 11.2 hands high, the Shetland pony is a testament to the concept that greatness comes in small packages. Its compact build, adorned with a luxurious mane and tail, portrays elegance despite its modest stature.

Originating from the Shetland Isles, these ponies have been molded by centuries of natural selection in a rugged and demanding environment. Their sturdy frames and thick coats are a hints of their resilience and ability to thrive in challenging climates.

The Shetland pony's unique ability to adapt to its surroundings is closely tied to its historical breeding. These ponies were integral to life on the Shetland Isles, serving as pack animals, working in agriculture, and even pulling carts and carriages. This history of practical use has instilled in them a cooperative nature and an intelligent disposition.

Despite their small size, Shetland ponies possess remarkable strength and endurance. Their sturdy legs and surefootedness make them adept at navigating diverse terrains, while their gentle demeanor makes them excellent companions for children and adults alike.

The Shetland pony's contributions extend beyond the farm and into the realm of equestrian sports. These ponies have showcased their agility and versatility in various disciplines, including driving, jumping, and dressage. Their small stature and strong work ethic have made them popular choices for therapy programs and as guide animals for the visually impaired.

Famous examples of Shetland ponies include "Piper's Brae Golden Flute," an accomplished driving pony, and "Wix of Berry," who held the Guinness World Record for the smallest pony in terms of height.

Shire Horse
Majestic Giant

The Shire horse, a majestic giant with a rich history, possesses a remarkable blend of characteristics that have made it a true icon of strength and reliability. The Shire has an imposing stature but a noble demeanour.

Standing at an impressive height of 16 to 17.2 hands high, the Shire horse commands attention with its grandeur. Its muscular and robust frame, built for heavy labour, reflects the result of selective breeding over generations. This breed's imposing presence has earned it a place of honor in parades, shows, and working demonstrations.

The Shire's distinct appearance is characterised by its feathered legs, a feature that harkens back to its historical role as a working draft horse. These long, silky feathers add an element of elegance to its powerful form, setting it apart from other breeds.

One of the most remarkable aspects of the Shire horse is its history of breeding. Originating in England, this breed emerged from the need for strong and capable horses to perform a range of agricultural and industrial tasks. Over time, careful breeding efforts have refined its qualities, resulting in a horse with unmatched strength and versatility.

The Shire's utility in agriculture and industry has left an indelible mark on human progress. These horses were instrumental in plowing fields, hauling heavy loads, and powering machinery during the industrial revolution. Their unwavering work ethic and power have shaped societies and contributed to technological advancement.

Famous Shire horses have made notable achievements that showcase their capabilities. One such example is "Dolly," a Shire mare known for her impressive strength. In 1810, Dolly pulled a load weighing 15 tons, earning her a place in history as a testament to the breed's sheer power.

In more recent times, Shire horses have participated in competitive events, demonstrating their prowess beyond their traditional roles. These events often include pulling contests, where Shires showcase their incredible strength and teamwork by hauling weighted sleds.

Tennesse Walking Horse
Unique Four-Beat Running-Walk

The Tennessee Walking Horse or Tennessee Walker is a breed of gaited horse known for its unique four-beat running-walk and flashy movement. It was originally developed as a riding horse on farms and plantations in the American South. It is a popular riding horse due to its calm disposition, smooth gaits and sure-footedness.

Standing at an average height of 15 to 16 hands high, the Tennessee Walking Horse boasts an elegant and well-proportioned physique. Its refined build and a sleek profile reflects a sense of both power and poise.

One of the Tennessee Walking Horse's most defining features is its signature gait—the "running walk." This smooth and gliding gait, characterised by the horse's nodding head and four-beat rhythm, offers an incredibly comfortable and effortless ride for the rider. This unique gait, innate to the breed, sets the Tennessee Walking Horse apart from others and has made it a sought-after choice for pleasure riding and shows.

The breed's history is deeply tied to the American South. Developed in the late 19th century, the Tennessee Walking Horse evolved from various breeds, including Thoroughbreds, Morgans, and Standardbreds. The goal was to create a versatile and comfortable riding horse that could cover long distances with ease—a testament to the practical needs of the time.

In the realm of equestrian artistry, the Tennessee Walking Horse shines in various show competitions, particularly in "gaited" events. Its distinctive running walk, coupled with its elegant presence, has earned it numerous accolades and medals in the show ring. The breed's ability to effortlessly perform this gait showcases the harmony between horse and rider and underscores its role as a true partner in the equestrian world.

Famous Tennessee Walking Horses have made their mark through outstanding achievements. One notable example is "Midnight Sun," a legendary stallion known for his exceptional running walk and graceful presence. Midnight Sun's influence in the breed's development is profound, and he is celebrated as a cornerstone of the Tennessee Walking Horse lineage.

Dartmoor Pony
Hardy & Windswept

The Dartmoor Pony is a breed of ponies that live in Devon, England. The breed has been in England for centuries and is used in a variety of roles. Because of the extreme weather conditions experienced on the moors, the Dartmoor Pony is a particularly hardy breed with excellent stamina.

Standing at a smaller height of 11.2 to 12.2 hands high, the Dartmoor Pony presents a compact and sturdy frame that reflects its roots in the rugged terrain of the Dartmoor region in southwestern England. Its robust build and well-proportioned physique are a result of centuries of adaptation to the challenging environment.

The Dartmoor's coat, known for its resilience and weatherproof qualities, showcases an array of colours, including bay, brown, grey, and occasionally, black. This natural camouflage serves as a tribute to its ability to seamlessly blend into the diverse moorland landscape.

A defining feature of the Dartmoor Pony is its exceptional hardiness. Developed over generations, this breed has thrived in the harsh conditions of Dartmoor's open moors, enduring wind, rain, and snow. This resilience, rooted in centuries of natural selection, underscores the breed's adaptability and survival instincts.

The Dartmoor Pony is characterised by its intelligence but independent spirit. Despite its wild origins, it can form strong bonds with humans through patient and respectful handling. Its curiosity and willingness to engage in activities make it a versatile partner.

Breeding programs aimed at preserving the Dartmoor Pony's genetic heritage have contributed to the breed's continued presence. These efforts focus on maintaining the breed's natural hardiness and adaptability, while also ensuring its suitability for modern roles such as riding, driving, and conservation grazing.

While the Dartmoor Pony is not often associated with competitive events, its historical role and enduring presence have earned it a place of distinction. Dartmoor Ponies have become ambassadors for the natural beauty of the moorlands, embodying the free spirit of the untamed wilderness.

Fresian
Graceful & Nimble Breathtaking Movement

The Friesian (also Frizian) is a horse breed originating in Friesland, in the Netherlands. Although the conformation of the breed resembles that of a light draught horse, Friesians are graceful and nimble for their size. It is believed that during the Middle Ages, ancestors of Friesian horses were in great demand as war horses throughout continental Europe.

Standing with a regal height of 14.2 to 17 hands, the Friesian horse commands attention with its striking appearance. Its noble head, adorned with a flowing mane and a luxuriant tail, creates a portrait of true equine magnificence.

The Friesian's heritage traces back to the Netherlands, where it was selectively bred over centuries. Rooted in the Friesland province, this breed has evolved through careful lineage management to maintain its distinctive traits. Its distinctive black coat, often glistening with a sheen reminiscent of polished ebony, is a hallmark feature.

This breed's movement is nothing short of breathtaking. The Friesian horse possesses powerful, high-stepping gaits that exude grace and allure. Its athleticism shines in dressage, where its natural ability to collect, extend, and perform intricate movements makes it a standout performer in the arena.

A true testament to the Friesian horse's versatility is its dual role as a driving horse. Adorned in ornate harnesses, these horses effortlessly pull carriages in elegant parades and events, harking back to a bygone era of grandeur and sophistication.

The Friesian horse's temperament is equally noteworthy. Known for its gentle disposition and willingness to work, it forms deep bonds with its riders. Its intelligence and eagerness to please make it a popular choice for various equestrian disciplines, from dressage to pleasure riding.

Gypsy Vanner
The traveller

The Gypsy Vanner, also known as the Traditional Gypsy Cob, Irish Cob, Romani Cob, Gypsy Horse is breed of domestic horse from the islands Great Britain and Ireland.

Bred by the Romani people, these horses were meticulously selected for their utility and splendor. The breed's name itself, "Gypsy Vanner," reflects its dual nature: "Gypsy" pays homage to its Romani origins, while "Vanner" signifies its role as a versatile draft and carriage horse.

Standing at an average height of 14 to 16 hands high, the Gypsy Vanner is renowned for its sturdy build and abundant feathering adorning its legs. Its strikingly beautiful coat, a canvas of vibrant colors and patterns, is a hallmark feature that captures attention wherever it treads.

The Gypsy Vanner's versatile nature is as impressive as its appearance. It possesses a natural affinity for driving, showcasing its power and elegance in various carriage events. Beyond its prowess as a driving horse, the Gypsy Vanner excels in riding disciplines, captivating riders with its comfortable gaits and gentle demeanor.

Famous Gypsy Vanner examples have not only embodied the breed's attributes but have also achieved recognition on the global stage. One such luminary is "The Gypsy King," a stallion whose exceptional conformation and movement have earned him numerous championships, awards, and a legacy as a breed ambassador. Another notable figure is "Cushti Bok," who became a crowd favorite with his incredible jumping ability and charismatic presence.

Stories of Gypsy Vanners have woven themselves into equestrian lore, and these horses often grace parades and festivals, evoking a sense of wonder and nostalgia. Their connection with the Romani people, known for their close bond with horses, adds an aura of mystique to their legacy.

In recent years, Gypsy Vanners have found their place in therapeutic programs, where their gentle disposition and striking appearance offer solace and companionship to individuals facing physical and emotional challenges.

Haflinger
Avelignese

The Haflinger, also known as the Avelignese, is a breed of horse developed in Austria and northern Italy

The haflinger has a smaller standing height of 13.2 to 15 hands high, but has compact strength and sturdy elegance. Its well-proportioned build, characterized by a broad chest, strong legs, and a short back, reflects the breed's origins in the Alpine mountains.

The Haflinger's most recognisable feature is its luscious, flowing mane and tail, which often cascade in shades of flaxen gold. This characteristic adds to its captivating charm, making it an ideal choice for parades and exhibitions.

Originating in the picturesque valleys of the South Tyrolean Alps, the Haflinger horse carries a rich legacy of utility and hard work. Bred by monks in the Middle Ages, it was refined over centuries for its ability to navigate rugged terrain, haul carts, and serve as a loyal farm companion.

In addition to its history as a dependable workhorse, the Haflinger has showcased its remarkable versatility in modern times. It has found success in various equestrian disciplines, including dressage, driving, and even jumping. This adaptability highlights the breed's innate intelligence and willingness to learn.

The Haflinger's gentle temperament further adds to its appeal. It is known for its amiable and cooperative nature, making it a wonderful partner for riders of all ages and skill levels. Its friendly disposition fosters a strong bond with its human companions, enhancing the overall equestrian experience.

One of the most famous Haflinger horses is "Nobleman of Tudor Oaks," affectionately known as "Noble." This exceptional Haflinger achieved international recognition in the sport of combined driving. Under the guidance of driver Suzy Stafford, Noble won multiple national championships and represented the United States in international competitions, including the FEI World Driving Championships for Singles.

Selle Français
Bred for sport

The Selle Français is a breed of sport horse from France. It is renowned primarily for its success in show jumping, but many have also been successful in dressage and eventing. An athletic horse with good gait.

Standing at an average height of 15.3 to 17.3 hands high, the Selle Français boasts a harmonious and athletic build. Its well-proportioned physique reflects generations of meticulous breeding with a focus on performance and conformation.

At the heart of the Selle Français' success is its exceptional lineage. Bred for sport, this breed is the result of strategic crossings, often involving Thoroughbreds, Arabians, and native French breeds. This careful blending of bloodlines has yielded a horse with remarkable speed, agility, and endurance.

One of the most remarkable traits of the Selle Français is its versatility. With a focus on show jumping, dressage, and eventing, this breed excels across a range of disciplines. Its fluid and expressive gaits, coupled with a natural athleticism, make it a sought-after choice for competitive riders.

Temperamentally, the Selle Français horse possesses a remarkable blend of intelligence, willingness, and responsiveness. Its amiable nature, combined with a strong work ethic, establishes a solid partnership between rider and horse, fostering a harmonious relationship based on mutual trust.

Famous examples of the Selle Français' prowess are abundant. Notably, Jappeloup, a Selle Français gelding, achieved international stardom alongside rider Pierre Durand. Together, they clinched the individual gold medal in show jumping at the 1988 Seoul Olympics, capturing the hearts of equestrian enthusiasts worldwide.

Additionally, the Selle Français breed has consistently earned medals in various equestrian competitions, including the Olympics, World Equestrian Games, and European Championships. These achievements stand as a testament to the breed's exceptional talent and the dedication of its riders and trainers.

Kathiawari

The Indian Desert War Horse

The Kathiawari or Kathiawadi is an Indian breed of horse. It originates in the Kathiawar peninsula of Gujarat in western India, and is associated with the Kathi people of that area. It was originally bred as a desert war horse for use over long distances, in rough terrain, on minimal rations.

Standing at shorter average height of 14.2 to 15.2 hands, the Kathiawari horse presents a compact and sturdy frame that exemplifies its endurance and resilience.

The Kathiawari's coat comes in a spectrum of colours, from dazzling white to chestnut, black, and even the rare silver dun. These hues mirror the diverse landscapes of the region, underscoring the breed's deep connection to its native land.

Beyond its striking appearance, the Kathiawari horse exhibits a remarkable combination of strength and agility. Its gaits are fluid and comfortable, a reflection of its historical use as a versatile workhorse and an esteemed companion for cavalry purposes.

The Kathiawari's temperament echoes its roots as a loyal and trustworthy partner. Known for its gentle disposition and intelligence, it forms strong bonds with its riders and handlers, showcasing an innate willingness to collaborate.

Breeding and preservation efforts have played a crucial role in ensuring the Kathiawari horse's continued existence. Organizations and enthusiasts have worked diligently to maintain the breed's purity and cultural significance, safeguarding a living testament to India's equestrian heritage.

Famous examples of the Kathiawari horse are not only prized for their physical prowess but also for their historic feats. These horses have excelled in endurance races, traversing vast distances with remarkable stamina. Some notable Kathiawaris have been awarded medals and accolades, showcasing their impressive achievements in equestrian competitions.

British Thoroughbred
Speed & Elegance

The British Thoroughbred horse, is bred for speed, elegance, and competitive prowess, it embodies a unique blend of heritage, breeding excellence, and remarkable achievements.

Standing at an average height of 15 to 17 hands high, the British Thoroughbred is a majestic equine specimen that exudes an aura of power and grace. Its well-defined musculature and slender build are a testament to generations of selective breeding aimed at maximising speed and agility.

The British Thoroughbred's bloodlines trace back to the 17th and 18th centuries, when breeders meticulously selected horses for their remarkable speed and endurance. This careful selection process gave rise to a breed known for its natural aptitude for racing and its ability to excel in the world of equestrian sports.

At the heart of the British Thoroughbred's legacy lies its unparalleled achievements in horse racing. The breed's innate speed, combined with its competitive spirit, has resulted in numerous victories on racetracks around the world. One of the most famous examples is the legendary racehorse "Secretariat," who, though an American Thoroughbred, captured the hearts of millions with his astounding victories, including a Triple Crown win in 1973.

In the realm of British Thoroughbred racing, the horse "Frankel" shines as a modern icon. Unbeaten in all 14 of his races, Frankel's flawless career has solidified his status as one of the greatest racehorses of all time.

Furthermore, British Thoroughbreds have consistently dominated prestigious events like the Epsom Derby, the Grand National, and the Royal Ascot, showcasing their unparalleled prowess on the track.

The British Thoroughbred's legacy is not confined to the racetrack. It is also found in The Household Cavalry in the United Kingdom, The horses used by the Household Cavalry are selected for their height, conformation, and temperament, and then undergo rigorous training to become part of the world-renowned mounted ceremonial units.

Connemara Pony
Distinctly Irish

The Connemara region in County Galway in western Ireland, where the breed first became recognised as a distinct type, is a very harsh landscape, thus giving rise to a pony breed of hardy, strong individuals. Some believe that the Connemara developed from Scandinavian ponies that the Vikings first brought to Ireland.

Standing between 12.2 to 14.2 hands high, the Connemara Pony's stature belies its impressive capabilities. Its well-proportioned frame, often cloaked in a dense, weather-resistant coat, reflects its origins in the challenging landscapes of western Ireland.

The Connemara's origins trace back to a fusion of native pony breeds with influences from Arabian, Thoroughbred, and Andalusian bloodlines. This deliberate breeding has imbued the Connemara Pony with exceptional endurance, agility, and a kind and willing temperament.

The breed's coat colour can vary, encompassing a range from grey, dun, bay, and black, to roan and palomino. The Connemara's striking appearance is enhanced by its well-chiseled head, kind eyes, and alert ears, creating a visage that exudes intelligence and character.

One of the Connemara's most impressive attributes is its versatility. Renowned for its prowess in both riding and driving, the Connemara excels in an array of disciplines, including dressage, show jumping, eventing, and endurance riding. This adaptability has earned it recognition as a true all-rounder.

Famous Connemara Ponies have etched their names into equestrian history. One notable example is Dexter Leam Pondi, a Connemara stallion that achieved remarkable success in the sport of eventing. With multiple wins at international events and prestigious medals, Dexter Leam Pondi exemplifies the breed's excellence in equestrian competition.

Yonaguni
Small But Loyal Japanese Breed

The Yonaguni or Yonaguni uma is a critically-endangered Japanese breed of small horse. It is native to Yonaguni Island, in the Yaeyama Islands in south-western Japan, close to Taiwan. It is one of eight horse breeds native to Japan.

Standing at an average height of 11.2 to 12.2 hands high, the Yonaguni horse embodies a compact yet sturdy frame that speaks to its resilience in the face of challenging environments and the breed's ability to thrive amidst the island's rugged terrain.

The Yonaguni horse's coat, often a rich bay or chestnut hue, showcases a natural harmony with its surroundings.

A key hallmark of the Yonaguni horse is its adaptability. Shaped by centuries of living in harmony with the island's conditions, this breed possesses a remarkable ability to navigate rocky landscapes and endure the climatic variations that define Yonaguni Island.

The Yonaguni horse's role in Japanese culture is intertwined with its utilitarian function. Historically, these horses were indispensable partners for local fishermen, assisting in the transportation of heavy fishing nets and equipment across the island's challenging terrain.

Though its presence on the international equestrian stage may be less prominent, the Yonaguni horse has captured the admiration of those who value cultural preservation and unique equine heritage. While specific achievements and medals may not be widely documented, the Yonaguni horse's significance lies in its role as a living embodiment of the enduring bond between humans and animals, particularly in the context of local traditions.

New Forest Pony
A Native Pony Breed Of The British Isles

The New Forest pony is one of the recognised mountain and moorland or native pony breeds of the British Isles.

Standing at an average height of 12 to 14.2 hands high, the New Forest Pony exudes a sense of rustic charm. Its sturdy and well-proportioned build reflects generations of selective breeding, resulting in a versatile and reliable equine partner.

The origins of the New Forest Pony trace back centuries, shaped by the historical traditions of the New Forest region. A product of natural selection and human stewardship, these ponies have thrived in the diverse landscapes that characterise their homeland.

One of the most distinctive features of the New Forest Pony is its remarkable coat, which comes in a variety of colours, from bay and grey to chestnut and roan. This adaptability in coloration aids its ability to blend seamlessly into its natural surroundings.

Beneath its enchanting exterior lies a pony with an amiable and gentle temperament. The New Forest Pony is known for its friendly disposition, making it an ideal companion for riders of all ages, from children to adults. Its intelligence and willingness to learn contribute to its reputation as a versatile and trainable breed.

The New Forest Pony's versatility extends beyond its temperament to its performance capabilities. A proficient and willing participant in various disciplines, from riding and driving to showing and jumping, this breed demonstrates an innate aptitude for adapting to different activities.

Historically, the New Forest Pony has been a beloved presence in British equestrian culture. Its contributions to agricultural work, transportation, and even wartime efforts have solidified its place in the annals of equine history.

Suffolk Punch
Tall & Mighty

The Suffolk Horse, also historically known as the Suffolk Punch or Suffolk Sorrel, is an English breed of draught horse. The first part of the name is from the county of Suffolk in East Anglia, and the word "Punch" is an old English word for a short stout person

The Suffolk Punch horse is a sight to behold, exuding a sense of awe with its massive yet well-proportioned frame. Towering between 16 to 17.2 hands high, it is among the tallest of heavy horse breeds. Its muscular build, with a distinctively broad chest and sturdy legs, reflects its origins as a working partner in the fields of East Anglia.

What truly distinguishes the Suffolk Punch is its rich chestnut coat, often accompanied by a distinct flaxen mane and tail. This striking coloration adds a touch of elegance to its robust appearance, creating an arresting contrast that draws attention to its magnificence.

The Suffolk Punch's origins trace back to the fertile farmlands of England. Developed in the early 16th century, this breed emerged through a careful and purposeful breeding process aimed at creating a robust and powerful horse for farm labour. It is a reflection of generations of agricultural ingenuity, a living legacy of the hardworking horses that once powered the fields.

This breed's influence extends beyond the plow and the field, as it has garnered acclaim for its strength and versatility. In the early 20th century, the Suffolk Punch gained recognition for its participation in competitive pulling contests. These feats of strength often led to triumphs in local fairs and agricultural shows, showcasing the breed's ability to pull astounding weights with unwavering determination.

Among the Suffolk Punch's distinguished achievements, perhaps none shines brighter than the story of "Young Tyrant." This remarkable stallion, born in 1909, was celebrated for his unparalleled strength and work ethic. His prowess in the pulling arena earned him numerous medals and awards, solidifying his place as a legendary figure in the breed's history.

Budyonny
From The Russian Revolution

The Budyonny was named after Marshal Semyon Budyonny, a Bolshevik cavalry commander who became famous during the Russian Revolution. The breed was created by Budyonny, a well-known horse breeder himself, in the early 1920s.

Standing proudly at around 15.2 to 16.2 hands high, the Budyonny Horse is characterised by its well-proportioned physique, balanced and harmonious. With a muscular frame of strength and power, it encapsulates the essence of a working horse that has played a pivotal role in various domains.

The Budyonny's coat is typically solid in colour, ranging from chestnut to bay and occasionally gray. This straightforward elegance, combined with its refined head and expressive eyes, imparts a regal air to the breed, reflecting its esteemed place in history.

Bred with a distinct purpose, the Budyonny Horse was developed in the early 20th century by crossing the Don horse, Thoroughbred, and a variety of other breeds. This careful breeding program sought to create a versatile equine capable of excelling in various equestrian disciplines while maintaining the strength and endurance required for military and agricultural tasks.

Notably, the Budyonny Horse has carved its name into the annals of equestrian history through its achievements and accolades. The breed has proven itself in a range of disciplines, from dressage and show jumping to eventing and racing. Its natural athleticism, intelligence, and willingness to perform have earned it medals and recognition on international stages.

One renowned example is the Budyonny mare "Belyanka," whose exceptional performance in dressage garnered her numerous accolades, including a gold medal at the 1980 Summer Olympics in Moscow. This remarkable achievement not only showcased the breed's versatility but also solidified its place in the pantheon of equestrian excellence.

Sandalwood Pony
From the Badlands

The Sandalwood Pony is a breed of small horse originating from Indonesia, on the Sumba and Sumbawa Islands. It is named after the Sandalwood trees, which are a major export of the country. The Sandalwood pony is one of the finest in the country, partly due to the great amount of Arabian blood. They make suitable children's ponies, and have been exported to Australia for this purpose.

Standing at a shorter average height of 11 to 12.2 hands high, the Sandalwood pony showcases a unique combination of strength and elegance and sense of grace that belies its smaller size.

One of the defining features of the Sandalwood pony is its adaptability to the varied landscapes of India. The breed's versatility is a direct result of its historical role as a reliable companion for local communities. This adaptability is complemented by its sturdy legs, agile movements, and an innate ability to navigate challenging terrains.

The Sandalwood pony's coat exhibits a wide range of colours, from bay and chestnut to grey and even pinto patterns. This diversity of colours mirrors the breed's historical purpose, which encompassed a spectrum of tasks, from agricultural work to transportation.

The Sandalwood pony typically has s a gentle disposition and willingness to work alongside humans. Its cooperative nature and inherent intelligence make it an ideal partner for a multitude of activities.

In competitive circles, the Sandalwood pony may not have garnered international fame, but its significance lies in its unwavering service and loyalty. These qualities, which have been honed through centuries of partnership, have undoubtedly contributed to the breed's enduring legacy within the cultural mosaic of India.

Nokota
From the Badlands

The Nokota horse is a feral and semi-feral horse breed located in the badlands of southwestern North Dakota in the United States. The breed developed in the 19th century from foundation bloodstock consisting of ranch-bred horses produced from the horses of local Native Americans mixed with Spanish horses, Thoroughbreds, harness horses and related breeds.

Standing at an average height of 14 to 15 hands high, the Nokota Horse's sturdy frame and compact build reflect its evolution in the unforgiving landscapes of North Dakota.

The Nokota's coat, which can vary from solid colours to striking patterns, hints at its diverse lineage. Rooted in the historic horses of Native American tribes and early settlers, the Nokota's coat patterns pay homage to the breed's mixed heritage and the melding of cultures on the American frontier.

The Nokota's bloodline is a tapestry woven with the stories of indigenous peoples and pioneers. Efforts to preserve the breed's unique characteristics have led to its recognition and distinction as an American heritage breed.

The Nokota Horse's versatility and adaptability make it a true treasure of the American West. Its endurance, intelligence, and willingness to collaborate have made it a reliable companion for ranching, trail riding, and even competitive events.

The Nokota's legacy is intertwined with tales of wild horse herds that once roamed the Badlands, evoking images of freedom and untamed landscapes. While not as widely recognised as some other breeds, individual Nokota Horses have left their mark in competitive arenas and trail riding events, showcasing the breed's diverse talents.

In recent years, the Nokota Horse's historical significance has been recognised and celebrated. Dedicated individuals have worked tirelessly to ensure the preservation of this unique breed, and their efforts have led to increased awareness and appreciation for the Nokota's heritage.

Irish Sport Horse
Built For Speed & Purpose

The Irish Sport Horse, or Irish Hunter, is an Irish breed of warmblood sporting horse, used mostly for dressage, eventing and show-jumping. It was bred from 1923 by cross-breeding of Irish Draught and Thoroughbred stock. There was some limited intromission of Hanoverian, Selle Français and Trakehner blood in the 1990s It is a recognised true breed

Ranging in height from 15 to 17 hands high, the Irish Sport Horse boasts a well-proportioned frame that shouts power and elegance. This breed is the result of a carefully cultivated lineage, often featuring Thoroughbred, Irish Draught, and other warmblood influences. This careful blending yields a horse with an agile and athletic build, primed for success in various disciplines.

The Irish Sport Horse's coat comes in an array of colours, reflecting its diverse genetic heritage. The breed's adaptability is evident in its ability to thrive in the challenging climates of Ireland, a testament to its hardiness and resilience.

Notably, the breed's breeding programs emphasise the development of a horse capable of excelling in multiple equestrian pursuits. The infusion of Thoroughbred blood brings speed, endurance, and refinement, while the Irish Draught contribution adds strength, temperament, and surefootedness. The result is a horse that thrives in eventing, show jumping, dressage, and even hunting.

The Irish Sport Horse has proudly demonstrated its prowess on the international stage. In the realm of eventing, the breed has achieved remarkable success. Notable achievements include medal wins in Olympic Games, World Equestrian Games, and European Championships. These accolades highlight the breed's versatility and aptitude for excelling across a range of challenging competitions.

Famous examples of the Irish Sport Horse's achievements include horses like "Custom Made," ridden by David O'Connor, who clinched individual gold at the 2000 Sydney Olympics. Additionally, "Horseware Bushman," ridden by Mark Todd, contributed to numerous victories, earning both horse and rider a place in equestrian history.

Pottok
Endangered Ancient Breed

Pottok is an endangered, semi-feral breed of pony native to the Pyrenees of the Basque Country in France and Spain.

Standing at an average height of 11.2 to 13.2 hands high, the Pottok horse possesses a compact and robust physique, perfectly adapted to the rugged terrain of the Basque Country.

The Pottok's coat is a canvas of nature's palette, ranging from bay, black, and chestnut to the distinctive "pottoka" coloration, characterised by a mix of dark and light shades. This natural camouflage allows the Pottok to seamlessly blend into its surroundings.

What sets the Pottok breed apart is its unique breeding system. Historically, Pottok horses have been semi-feral, roaming freely in the mountains during the warmer months and returning to their villages in winter. This self-regulated breeding has resulted in a hardy and adaptable horse that embodies the essence of natural selection.

While not widely recognised on the global stage, the Pottok breed has produced notable individuals. The story of "Zaharrer Segi," a Pottok stallion, captured hearts as he carried a 9-year-old girl through the challenging mountain terrain to safety, a true testament to the breed's loyalty and surefootedness.

In recent years, the Pottok has gained attention for its versatility. It has excelled in equestrian sports such as dressage, jumping, and driving, showcasing its adaptability beyond its traditional roles.

Once common, it is endangered through habitat loss, mechanisation and crossbreeding but efforts are increasingly made to safeguard the future of this breed. It is considered iconic by the Basque people.

Akhal-Teke
The Golden Horse

Akhal-Teke is a Turkmen horse breed. They have a reputation for speed and endurance, intelligence, and a distinctive metallic sheen. The shiny coat of the breed led to their nickname, "Golden Horses".

Standing gracefully at an average height of 14.2 to 16 hands high, the Akhal-Teke's sleek and refined physique has an air of elegance. Its distinctive feature lies in its coat, which shimmers with a metallic sheen, reflecting light like a precious metal. This luminous quality, combined with its delicate head and fine features, makes the Akhal-Teke an exquisite sight to behold.

Originating from the arid lands of Turkmenistan, the Akhal-Teke has evolved through centuries of selective breeding. This breed's adaptability to the challenging desert environment is a testament to its resilience and hardiness. It possesses a refined bone structure and a well-defined musculature, contributing to its exceptional speed and agility.

The Akhal-Teke's gait is characterised by an effortless and fluid movement, lending itself to a range of disciplines. It is particularly celebrated for its prowess in endurance racing, a testament to its remarkable stamina and ability to cover vast distances with remarkable ease.

In the realm of breeding, the Akhal-Teke is renowned for its purity and bloodlines. The breed has been carefully preserved by Turkmen horsemen, who have safeguarded its heritage and maintained its distinctive qualities over generations.

Famous examples of the Akhal-Teke breed include:

Absent: A celebrated Akhal-Teke stallion known for his impressive achievements in endurance racing, including completing the 100-mile Tevis Cup multiple times.

Bay Abi: This legendary stallion was a world record holder in endurance, covering a staggering 214 kilometres (133 miles) in a single day in 1935.

Camargue
One Of The Oldest Breeds In the World

The Camargue horse is an ancient breed of horse indigenous to the Camargue area in southern France. Its origins remain relatively unknown, although it is generally considered one of the oldest breeds of horses in the world. For centuries, possibly thousands of years, these small horses have lived wild in the harsh environment of the Camargue marshes and wetlands of the Rhône delta,

Perhaps the most striking feature of the Camargue horse is its stunning coat. Born with a distinctive gray color, the coat lightens as the horse matures, eventually transforming into a luminous shade of white. This striking transformation reflects the breed's harmony with its surroundings and its ability to adapt to the changing seasons.

The origins of the Camargue horse trace back to ancient times, with a lineage deeply rooted in the annals of history. Bred in the wild and shaped by centuries of natural selection.

The Camargue horse's unique adaptability and surefootedness are a result of its upbringing in a challenging environment. Raised in the marshes and salt flats of the Camargue region, these horses have honed their ability to traverse treacherous terrains, making them exceptional companions for herding cattle and working alongside humans.

One of the most notable aspects of the Camargue horse's heritage is its integral role in the tradition of the gardians, the skilled herders of the Camargue. These horses are true partners to the gardians, aiding in the management of cattle and embodying the spirit of collaboration between human and horse.

Garrano
Endangered Breed Of Pack Horse

The Garrano is an endangered breed of pony from northern Spain and Portugal, part of the Iberian horse family, mainly used as a pack horse, for riding, and for light farm work. An ancient breed, the Garrano has remained largely unchanged for thousands of years but is in decline due to predation and loss of interest in breeding for agricultural use.

Standing at an average height of 11 to 13.2 hands high, the Garrano horse exhibits a charming blend of strength and agility within its compact frame. Its sturdy build, shaped by centuries of natural selection, reflects its ability to navigate rugged terrains and thrive in the demanding environments of the Portuguese mountains.

The Garrano's coat, which can range from bay and black to grey and dun, further exemplifies its close harmony with nature. This functional coloration provides camouflage amidst the rugged terrain and showcases its historical role as a working horse for local communities.

The Garrano horse demonstrates remarkable agility and endurance. Its gaits are characterized by fluidity and surefootedness, enabling it to navigate steep inclines and rocky paths with remarkable ease. This dexterity and stamina are essential qualities for the breed's traditional roles in herding, transportation, and agricultural work.

The Garrano's historical and cultural significance within Northern Portugal is profound. As a working companion of local communities, it has played an essential role in agriculture, herding, and transportation. This breed's legacy echoes the resilience of generations who have depended on it for survival in the challenging mountainous regions.

Standardbred
Master Of Harness Racing

The Standardbred is an American horse breed best known for its ability in harness racing, where members of the breed compete at either a trot or pace. Developed in North America, the Standardbred is recognized worldwide, and the breed can trace its bloodlines to 18th-century England. They are solid, well-built horses with good dispositions. In addition to harness racing, the Standardbred is used for a variety of equestrian activities, including horse shows and pleasure riding, particularly in the Midwestern and Eastern United States and in Southern Ontario.

Standing at an average height of 15 to 16 hands high, the Standardbred's well-balanced physique exudes an air of athleticism and strength. Its sturdy frame, defined by well-muscled shoulders and hindquarters, reflects its origins in harness racing and its capacity for sustained speed and power.

One of the defining features of the Standardbred is its pacing and trotting abilities. Distinct from other breeds, Standardbreds are bred specifically for their unique gait patterns, with trotters exhibiting a rhythmic diagonal gait and pacers showcasing a lateral gait. These gaits, honed through generations of selective breeding, are finely tuned for efficiency and speed.

The Standardbred's coat comes in a variety of colours, ranging from solid hues to striking pinto patterns. This diversity of coat colours mirrors the breed's adaptability and wide-ranging roles beyond racing tracks.

Beyond its physical attributes, the Standardbred boasts an inherent disposition of amiable and tractable nature. This affable temperament, has made it a choice for law enforcement and military roles around the world.

Finnhorse
The Official National Horse Breed Of Finland

The Finnhorse or Finnish Horse is a horse breed with both riding horse and draught horse influences and characteristics, and is the only breed developed fully in Finland. In English it is sometimes called the Finnish

Standing at an average height of 14 to 15 hands high, the Finnhorse exhibits a solid and well-proportioned strong physique, Its robust build, characterised by a sturdy frame and powerful limbs, reflects its origins as a working horse in demanding environments.

Rooted in a rich history of selective breeding, the Finnhorse is the collaborative efforts of Finnish breeders who aimed to create a versatile and adaptable equine companion. Over centuries, the breed has evolved into a true embodiment of Finnish identity, reflecting the nation's agricultural heritage and reliance on reliable equine partners.

The coat of the Finnhorse is often found in shades of chestnut, bay, and occasionally grey.

The Finnhorse's versatile nature shines through in its exceptional suitability for a wide range of tasks. From farm work and forestry to riding and even trotting races, the breed's adaptability and work ethic have earned it a revered status within Finland's equestrian traditions.

Notable achievements and stories further underscore the Finnhorse's significance. The breed's prowess in harness racing is particularly remarkable, with individuals like Viesker securing titles and accolades on both national and international stages. The Finnhorse's prowess in trotting competitions is a source of national pride, exemplifying its speed, endurance, and competitive spirit.

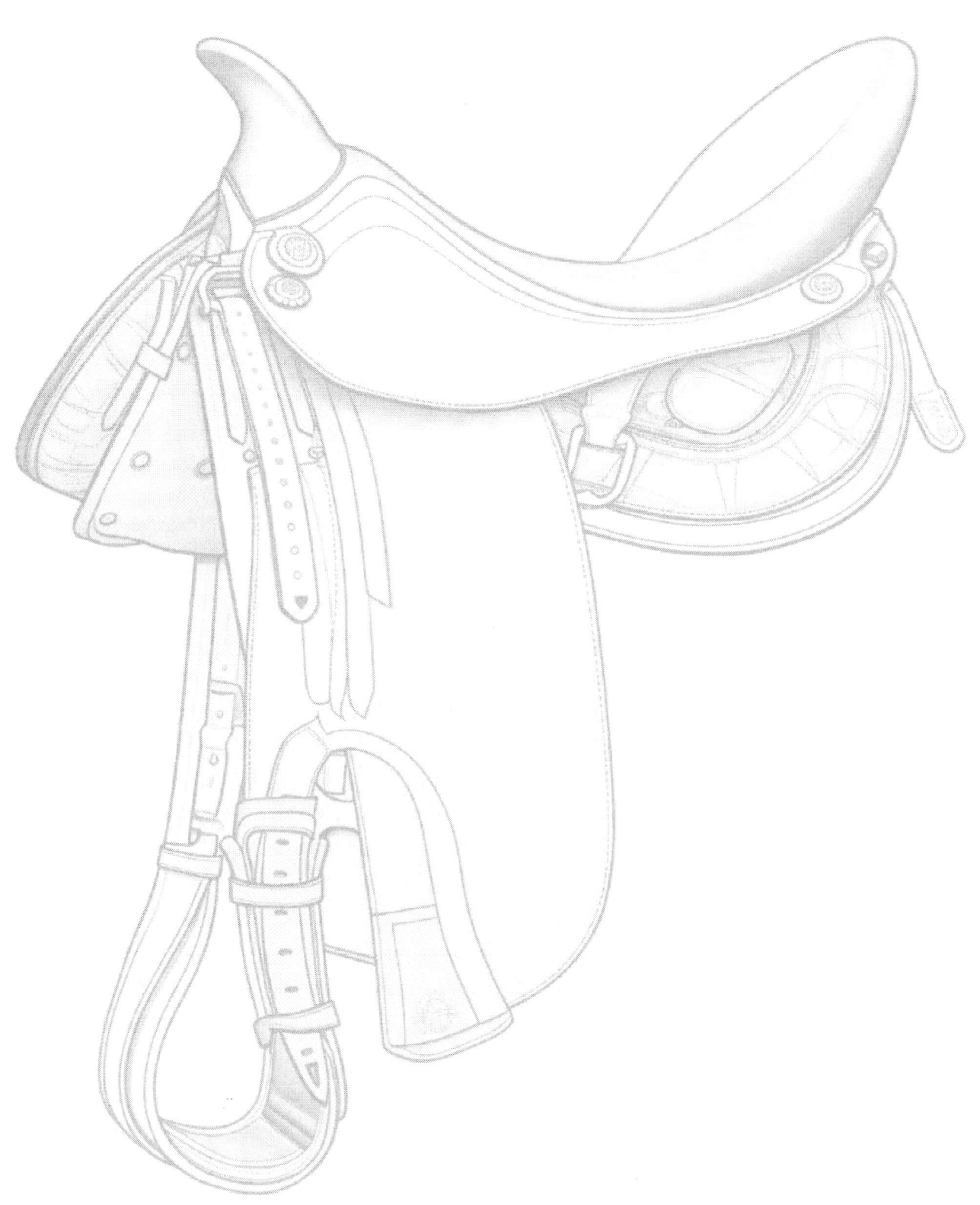

Printed in Great Britain
by Amazon

36324958R00064